STAGE **5**
BOOK 3

THE MISSING PLUMBER

John Townsend

RISING★STARS

"Pst ... listen. Can you hear it?" Roo spoke softly into Lee's ear. "Are you awake?"
He knocked gently on her bed.
"I am now," she groaned. "What time is it?"
"Just after midnight ... about half past if you must know," he sighed. "But listen. Can you hear tapping? I reckon it's a burglar."

"What do you want me to do about it?"
Lee moaned as she sat up in a daze.

"Come with me to take a look," Roo said in a whisper. "I'd better not disturb Dad. He's not been well so I doubt he'll wake up. It's up to us to sort this."

Lee was still half asleep as she wrapped a dressing gown around her shoulders.

She held Roo's arm tightly and they crept outside.
"Wait and listen," she hissed.

They stood very still and heard 'tap …
tap … tap …' from not far away.
Roo gave a gasp, "I knew it. It's Flat 51."

"This is wrong," Lee said. "If it's a robber, we must call the police."

"Keep calm, Lee," replied Roo. "It might not be a robber. It might be the plumber. I saw him last night, remember? We just need to check."

Roo crept slowly along the landing with Lee by his side.

Roo made a fist and tapped his knuckle. "I'll fight back and wrestle him to the ground," he said.

They got to the door of Flat 51. It was open, with a light inside. "I'm going in," Roo whispered. "You wait here. If it's OK, I'll give you the thumbs-up sign. If not, I'll yell." All was silent as he crept into Flat 51 ... and to the kitchen.

51

15

There were crumbs all over the floor. A knife was beside a toolbox.

"That looks like the plumber's spanner and wrench," Roo said to himself.

A broken tap dripped into a bucket of water. There was an old cooker with a wrecked oven door.

Then the tapping began again.
Tap ... tap ... tap ...

Roo ran back to find Lee by the lift. "That tapping is coming from in here," Lee said. She pressed the lift button and stood back.

The doors slid open and a man fell out. "At last," he panted. "I've been stuck in that lift for hours. The button jammed. My legs are numb. I didn't have my phone with me. I was just going to get my other spanner to fix the tap."

"So YOU are the plumber," Roo grinned. "You're the missing plumber with a talent for taps. You don't just fix them, you make loud ones in the night too!"

1. Why did Roo wake Lee?

2. Why didn't he wake Dad?

3. What did Lee think they should do?

4. Where did they go?

5. What did Roo see in the kitchen?

6. Where did Roo run?

7. Who was in the lift and why?

*Find the **verbs** to fill the gaps.*

1. She _____ a dressing gown around her shoulders.   (page 6)

2. She _____ Roo's arm tightly and they _____ outside.   (page 6)

3. "Wait and listen," she _____ .   (page 6)

What's missing?

1. i am now she groaned what time is it   (page 3)

2. simple roo said with a look of utter horror we run (page 12)

3. im going in roo whispered you wait here   (page 14)

*Find the **nouns** to fill the gaps.*

1. No _____ works this late.   (page 10)

2. I'll give you the _____-up sign.   (page 14)

3. There were _____ all over the floor.   (page 16)

WORD POWER

Which word in the story means

1. thief or robber?   (page 3)

2. mutter or mumble?   (page 10)

3. stuck or wedged?   (page 20)

4. gift or ability?   (page 21)

*Swap the word in **bold** for a new word that means the opposite.*

5. Roo spoke **softly** into Lee's ear.

6. She held Roo's arm **tightly**.

7. Lee croaked **weakly**.

8. Roo crept **slowly** along the landing.